The Better Angels of Our Nature

Poems by Jason Baldinger

Kung Fu Treachery Press
Rancho Cucamonga, CA
kungfutreachery@gmail.com

Copyright © Jason Baldinger, 2019
First Edition 1 3 5 7 9 10 8 6 4 2
ISBN: 978-1-950380-10-7
LCCN: 2019935729

Design, edits and layout: John T. Keehan, Jr.
Cover image: Jason Baldinger
Author photo: Ethan Meyer
All rights reserved. No part of this publication may be reproduced or transmitted in any form or by any means, electronic or mechanical, including photocopying, recording or by info retrieval system, without prior written permission from the author.

Some of the poems in this collection were published by *In-Between Hangovers, Heartland! Poems of Love, Resistance and Solidarity* and *Winedrunk Sidewalk, Red Fez* and *Rusty Truck*. Portions of the poem *Onragocracy* were heard in the song *Poor People are Revolting* by Sub-Pop recording artists The Gotobeds.

CONTENTS

A Change is Gonna Come / 1

Mary and the Future / 4

Thinking of Sand Creek / 6

Pints on Penn / 8

Résumé / 11

The Day Job / 15

The Better Angels of Our Nature / 17

Coda / 28

Lost and Absent Countries / 30

Poem for the Waitress at Red Robin / 32

Poem for James Baldwin / 35

Pooka / 36

A Cheeseburger on Memorial Day / 39

Elegy for the American Dream / 40

Hymn to Conspiracies / 42

A Hymn for the Surveillance State / 45

Postcard from Kimberling Lake / 47

To My Poet Friends on an American Holy Day / 49

On Finding Three Hundred Dollars in a Book on FDR
    That I Ordered off the Internet / 52

Lunch Time, Spahr Avenue / 53

Beefeaters / 55

Postcard from Bunker Hill / 57

Another Day in America / 58

Supplemental Nights / 59

Onagrocracy / 61

Hymn to the Greatest / 64

Talking God with Ussia / 66

A Fedora and a Mustache / 67

For Trane's Giant Steps / 70

Mr Pink Pussy Hat Salesman / 72

Three Views of High Street / 74

Hymn to Bloodsport / 76

March of the Infidels / 78

Kerouac Go Home / 80

Hey America
You could have had it any way you wanted it
You could have been a real democracy
You could have been free

        -Eugene McDaniels, *Love Letter to America*

Farewell my true love, farewell my fancy
Are you still owing me love, though you failed me?
But one last gesture for your pleasure
I'll paint your memory on the monument
In my rehearsal for retirement

        -Phil Ochs, *Rehearsals for Retirement*

A Change is Gonna Come

bar trivia, the seat between
a place for leaning as we
not playing, debate answers
tired of the lean, I move next to her

I can't remember what she did
her tech-bro boyfriend works too much
she moved with him from Philly
she stays in bars, he works
she comes home when he does
nothing clearer, she's lonely

she tells me one of her first memories
1992, her parents' Armenian immigrants
celebrating their home country independence

the Democratic National Convention on
Joe Biden as a patent leather sofa
spits vitriol at coming fascism
…
fascism
oligarchy
independence
freedom
from this far down the ladder
they might be words plucked out of a dream

it can't happen here
it can't happen here
I'm not sure that it's not happening here

2008
Shepard Fairey posters
hope and change
I watched election results at The Cage
drinking with friends
when Obama was announced president
the bar went mad
we felt change was real
we bought drinks
hugged and kissed
strangers and friends
naïve in hope
that change was gonna come
everybody banked it would be at least Sam Cooke
I hoped it would be Baby Huey

we got neither
four years then eight
of subverted democracy
of marginally better

I drive home considering
John McQueen, South Carolina Secessionist
to paraphrase; *white men rule our destinies*

as a country we fought a war over that
one hundred and fifty years later
we have a candidate who says it again
loudly, a buffoon, I'm embarrassed
embarrassed to call myself American

I bet too much on that change years ago
maybe that change was bigger
a simple tenet that this country was founded on
all men, nix, all persons are created equal
something future persons will wince at, not understanding
how we didn't believe it instinctively, inherently
it seems strange this is still a discussion
a discussion that makes any change an illusion

Mary and the Future

talking with Mary between breaks, Banjo Night
I was to meet her husband here
he's having a meltdown, American politics has him boiling
I understand, I've had fluttering
in my abdomen since the election
I can't escape these conversations
I don't want to escape these conversations
it seems all the gatherings I'm at
teeter at the point of toppling
we celebrate excesses now for an uncertain future
we dread an uncertain future
we prepare for the worst
we ask difficult moral questions
we are all outright frightened
Mary is no different
I'm no different

the conversation with Mary echoes many
what are we doing, what can we do, how do we do
NOW!
I say the same thing, it's so fucking American
instant gratification, most of us asleep
while our country, slowly commandeered
by robber barons, fascists, by a class of people who
serve only themselves, who pay politicians to serve them.

no one wants to admit this is class war
it's a farce to believe
an Industrial Revolution will come again
now it's an automated revolution
as such we should be working less for more
no one says that, like no one questioned before

we expect easy answers
there are no easy answers, never was
we've moved backwards, we keep going backwards

I say, Mary this is when as artists
as intellectuals, as advocates, as allies
this is the time to build our communities
as we should have been before
from the bottom up, this is how we'll shield our friends
this is how we'll inform those who haven't been
this how we start to change, start local
then merge into national
the law of inertia applies to humans
same as it applies to objects
now is the time for movement

Thinking of Sand Creek

today is the 152nd anniversary of the massacre at Sand Creek
I think of the Colorado desert, desolation, 103 degrees
it's May now, November then rushes through my head
as I survey the field, I can't breathe

I think tonight of Manzanar, the internment
of the Japanese, the desert overlooked
by Mount Whitney, sparse cabins once
jammed with persons, citizens, Americans
who were never found guilty of terrorism

I think tonight of Little Big Horn
           of Wounded Knee
              of Red Cloud's grandchildren
relegated to Pine Ridge Reservation
who painted above their meeting house door
The Indian Wars are far from over

there is a litany of cruelty
of hate within Americans
I've followed it around the country
Andersonville and prison camps north and south
battlefields, where blood was shed for freedom
I've crossed plantations and civil rights sites
I've looked for America's dirty secrets, its forgotten past
in out of the way places, always

believing we had passed
even as our government destabilizes
tampers around the world

now hate amplifies
open, oozing, not out of sight
I'm horrified, terrified, confused
somehow, we don't learn
what was relevant from our history
we learn what we want to believe

Pints on Penn

watching snow
from a second-floor bar
a reading, Christmas presents
in the window, strings of lights

today it was confirmed
I knew it was coming
laid off in a couple weeks
this is the second, maybe the third
year in a row I'm rolling the same scenario
I'm tired

I think over unemployment past
it comes with the winter
it comes more frequently

2000 was high on the hog
working twenty hours, fun-employment
if you will. I made more money
than I'd ever made, that's
the good old days now

05 was a fucking mess
no part time jobs, benefits had been cut
I did my best to stretch and pay
the rent while living out of bars

12 was running full speed
a season on the road milking
a severance package, figuring
it would all come together
it never did

14 was grilled cheese
twice a day, an Indian buffet
as a treat, a box of wine a week
and an unfinished novel
four people living in a one
bedroom apartment

last year it was living off
a princely sum for selling off
a nice jazz collection
last year it was losing my mind
my moorings, there was no way to keep still

today John Glenn died, rather than
wonder what's next, I think about
past Americas,
there seems to have
been a future once, we looked at stars
other worlds, even the working
class had optimism, each generation
built on the last those dreams
seem so far away now

consider my mother working
two jobs at 62, she raised me on social
security after my dad died, she put
herself through school at the same time
if that were an option now, it may not be anymore
she deserves better, we all do

still, I wonder what happened to those dreams
if anyone still dreams them
an Edward Bellamy world
a Eugene Debs world
a New Deal
a New Frontier
instead we get nightmares
instead we get the dawn of 1984

Résumé

dear human resources manager
I know you get millions of pieces of paper
from job hungry applicants
that you don't give a fuck about
much as we don't give a fuck about you
but capitalism hasn't ended
I mean it theoretically ended
when the Industrial Revolution was pronounced dead
but capital's endless exploitation is still rampant
apparently just to live
        just to experience life
is not an acceptable trade
I suppose it doesn't matter
that this is not meaningful work
there are mostly retail and service jobs
left for low-wage workers
who could only be so lucky
to dream about a universal basic income
or for that fact free health care
so I'll happily wait on Americans
who somehow believe that material possessions
will somehow fill the emptiness
in their hearts

I can't tell you what intangible qualities
I offer. I'm quick with new tasks
I've run businesses for friends dying of cancer

I work hard when there's work to be done
I think outside of the box
I like to write poems and daydream
I want to cry at least once a day
because the world is beautiful
because the world is sad
because I might be hungover
because existence is ultimately futile

I can tell you I won't spend more than
two hours a day in the bathroom
writing poems
on paper or on the stall walls
if I choose the walls
I promise you'll have
incredibly articulate customers
I'll even hide a dictionary
behind the toilet for customers to translate
because sometimes I get a penchant
to use a five-dollar word
I'll happily volunteer my Webster's
that I stole in eighth grade
it has space guns drawn in the margins
but it's served me well
for almost thirty years
I have no idea where I'll be in five years
in ten years, hell if any of us could see
that far into the future we wouldn't be sitting
here waiting for a fucking job
hell, I'm still not sure what I want to be

when I grow up, or maybe I know
but people don't pay poets money
people don't believe in art
people only believe
in money or a god that doesn't exist
they long for an afterlife
like I long for early retirement
I promise I won't say that out loud

I think it's safe to say I'm highly adaptable
last week I installed cabinets one day
hung a suspended ceiling the next
I sold records for friends in my spare time
I wrote and submitted poems
agreed to do another benefit show
then woke up and was a book mule
I drank beer on my break
because it tasted good
and I was tired and it was offered
and I learned a long time ago
that you should always say no
in moderation

seriously, I've sold paint to people
I've been cursed out for not having the key
to the narcotics locker when I managed a drug store
I pretended once to care about office supplies
sporting goods, deli meat, detailing cars
processing checks, auto parts
and that doesn't count all the things

that I may have pretended to care about
because I needed a job then
as I need a job now

I ask that if you drug test
I'll pass as long as you don't test for marijuana
I know it's still sort of illegal
I promise I won't smoke it before
a shift or in the middle of a shift
I do like it socially
generally, it's the only way
I get a good night's sleep
and that's important for productivity

that's what you want right
happy and productive workers
anesthetized and dreamless
wading through their lives
just getting by
constantly careening
at the drop edge of broke
a paycheck away from being hungry
a paycheck away from being homeless
a paycheck away from hope

The Day Job
(For Nancy Krieg)

we work till we're blind
figuratively perhaps
but when the garage door
goes up in darkness
comes down in darkness
it becomes hard
to tell if we haven't
accidentally transformed
into moles
and then the days bleed together
and together and together
until they become a river
we can't actually see
for having our heads
under, the paycheck
gets no bigger, we stretch
and stretch and stretch
to the point of breaking
it's a wonder we can even pretend
to be alright, all our heart
given out before we have time
to even rest with ourselves
of course, the world seems crazy
of course, it feels insurmountable

we wait, look for a magic wand
something to clear cloud cover
give you a few minutes to feel human
blank without the flow of the world
and with the sun directly on our faces
breathlessly easy for a short while

The Better Angels of Our Nature

The arc of the moral universe is long, but it bends towards justice.
-Martin Luther King

I

she was disturbed
noises at Camp Peary
Black Ops exercises
in the tideland woods
explosions, machine gun fire
Blackhawks beating moonlight
        beating clouds

she says this over drinks
in a bar that's gay one night a week
after we stopped at a candlelight protest

maybe some of the same kids are here now
some are her students
most not much older than we were
when we met forever ago

we haven't seen each other in years
catching up careers, life, miscellaneous debris
drunkenly talking out all the difficulties of family

the next day hung over, listless
on the couch, passing newspapers
she says I can play a record
we agree on silence
the world is dissonant enough

lately, real life resembles
all my five am anxiety dreams
the kind where I wake up
stare through the dark, wait for it to lift
the only thing pleasant
in those moments is silence

it's so hard to find silence
even in the comfort of friends
even while waiting
on the better angels of our nature

II

Big Star's *Third*
is crisp, clear
this ice sunshine morning

obsessed with *Take Care*
I play it over and again
long past Richmond
then switch to radio

I love radio
especially in some
huge American city
the mess of cultures
spills across am and fm dials
classic rock and mexicali polka
bollywood and gospel
raï and soul
hip hop and cumbia
classical and jazz
it bolsters me
   reminds me
what America is about

III

in a burger joint
my friends and I interrupted

Mark sweeps up here weekends along 6th
farther down the street weekdays

he says straight away
Donnie don't play that
we laugh, spark conversation

he doesn't understand
   can't accept

that it'll be alright
but being black
you get used to being ignored
        used to being harassed
        used to being stepped on
it's, excuse my language, he says
the fuckers who voted for him
that won't understand
how to live
when shit
rolls downhill on them

IV

the Library of Congress
the sum of our national knowledge
ceiling painted with quotes
statements
on freedom
on knowledge
on equality
and against tyranny

everything we've come to believe
or be misled about democracy
is here on display

everything knit
into our national fabric

is waiting
on the better
angels of our nature
to appear
drink
digest
and
practice

V

I stroll down the bluff
around the Capitol
there are persons of color
humans
today, mostly Muslim
holding signs in protest
milling after the event
I read signs as they pass
sometimes so intent on words
it seems I'm staring
when I notice, I smile wide
to acknowledge
your not alone
often relieved eyes
smile back at me

we are all immigrants
my family came from
Scotland via Toronto
when potato famines raged

my family came from Germany
when Wilson claimed
all Germans were the enemy
when it was good for business
as it always is, to go to war

my family came from Switzerland
looking for opportunity
this is what this country
was built on
since some rich white men
decided that freedom
was good for business

if you ban
Iranians, Iraqis, Somalis
Syrians, Libyans, Sundanese and Yemeni
I'll be happy
to add those nationalities
to my family tree

VI

Latina woman
in a wheelchair
pushed up the bluff
by her daughter
sign across her lap
Love Trumps Hate

daughter struggles
extended behind the chair
older woman
says something I can't hear
they both laugh
a joke that meant everything

VII

sunset at the Lincoln Memorial
wheelie kids fly across the mall
Muslims and sympathizers gather
a candlelight vigil

I need no help with The Gettysburg Address
it's burned in my heart
his second inaugural address
hits hardest

I knew I wouldn't hold back
how can you hold back tears
when a national tragedy is happening

the blood
not wrung from the lash
our sins
indelible

it seems to me
the Civil War
the Cold War
all of America's Endless Wars
are wars of attrition
no one wins

I take heart as I see people
take to the streets *en masse*
I take heart
when I see civil disobedience
protests peaceful and growing

jeremiads can be rewritten
by the better angels of our nature

further proof that government
of the people
by the people
for the people
shall not perish

VIII

the Vietnam Memorial
a wave in the dark

wheelie kids are home
Muslims on fire
the wind a bone saw

I have two uncles who served
neither killed in combat
one a casualty of alcohol
the toll quantified
years after he served two tours
the other still wears
shrapnel scars across his face

I don't believe in violence
I wonder now about that more
as I have conversations
I see more people who feel the same way
as I watch a government unconcerned
with the people it was to serve

it seems to me LBJ
believed in guns and butter
but guns beat butter
now it's only guns

fifty years after the wave crested
fifty years from where King's dream died
fifty years of an age of growing irrationalism
fifty years of violence, our national
jeremiad is one of blood
we've been wading deeply
it's stained every inch of this land

I stare through the dark
at lists of names
names of men
now gone

I am overwhelmed by the dead

IX

the fence is still up from Inauguration Day
it surrounds the White House
as do armed guards in digital camo

I was taught to believe
in god and country
in invisible hands and democracy

I have found no solace in god
choosing instead to believe in humanity
maybe, like Whitman, this is why
I can't give up on democracy

X

there is a feast waiting
in a basement apartment on D Street

beer we bought from a Korean bodega
chicken and mole
refried beans and rice
my friend's fiance's cooking is perfect

we talk about the places
our families came from
the stories we haven't lost
to time or being Americanized
we list all of the terrible things
we've seen and heard
in the name of freedom

freedom in our name
freedom cannot wait much longer
for the better angels of our nature

Coda

Arlington National Cemetery
I've walked fifteen miles in two days
maybe more, my legs are pegs
I've sprained my ankle
I don't have time for the tour
I decide to walk
        to limp to Kennedy's grave

I stare up at Robert E Lee's big house
they're refurbishing the slave cabins
making it undeniable,
the unbelievable cruelty of that era
which isn't that much different from this era

I watch the Eternal Flame a minute
listen to security guard hush
each person who speaks

I start back down the hill
my legs not working
the limp worse each step
I start for Medgar Evers grave
halfway, I feel like heading for the gate
stop, stare at the seventy degree
blue sky in January

rebuke myself
some gave all for freedom
Evers gave his life for it
a freedom all men should enjoy
a freedom that should be
self-evident

I keep on, steady stagger
find the grave easily
kneel, rest my head
no prayers
only silence

Lost and Absent Countries

five am, mind moves awake
more often now, part of getting older
anxiety takes over
other times, like tonight, it's the only time
to think without noise, except tinnitus

I'm lost reflecting on people
I haven't thought of, heard from in years
inventories of intersecting lines
time, decades in particular, become glaciers
stolen and absent countries

when I finally do drift
it's with Leonard Cohen lyrics
circling my head

that afternoon a friend texts
his brother died

I remember an old friend
when his father died
before cell phones, we talked via phone
drank port wine and whiskey
told stories of him
and his stories

until my friend was drunk enough
to take his grief with him
then it seemed like comfort
it seems now
we're left with staccato characters, empty screens
our rugged individualist myth
drowns itself isolated
misses a real connection

Poem for the Waitress at Red Robin

this evening its painfully clear
we are a nation of middle managers
purposeless and ineffectual
seated in cubicle booths
staring at cubicle buildings
doctor's offices architecture retail
doctor's office architecture town homes
decorated with blandly evocative Americana
spilled loudly across walls
it's my niece's birthday
I'm not about to reason
with a five-year-old why this place is awful

Rachel is our waitress
her name in black marker
droops in the same sad tired way
she carries herself
I don't know how many tables she has
the wait staff is jumping
feigning boisterous friendliness
except Rachel, who probably
goes home to kids and has to
try not to be too tired to take care of them

the food is worse than I remember
the tv over our head blares
the tv on the table tries to sell us games
the noise in the room throbs
dull crescendos, you can't hear the person
next to you, maybe we don't want to hear
the person next to us

my nephew has taken the toothpick
from my burger, says it's a sword
now it's a gun, he's fighting
imaginary bad guys

I take the toothpick
break it into three pieces
I ask *can we pretend*
there are no weapons
there are no bad guys
here is the state of Oklahoma
this is the state of Delaware
this is the Washington Monument
imagine a story where you're there
and there are no bad guys

instead it's a pistol
a sword and something else
this narrative is fed to us so young
maybe that's why so many Americans
fight bad guys that never existed

two ice cream sundaes have arrived
Rachel is back with three other waitresses
they sing happy birthday to my niece
because they have to
because it isn't life
        it isn't work
unless you get to demean yourself for tips

Poem for James Baldwin

reading Baldwin
in the well-lit bar
of a chain Italian joint

because I'm hungover
because shit service is everything
because his words are beautiful
because humans never learned how to be
    beautiful
because hope is too much
or because

the woman in her sixties
leans over leans in
touches my arm
asks
how's the chicken parmesan?

Pooka

(for Matt Borczon)

I've been doing a piss poor
Jimmy Stewart impersonation
him reading the first few lines of *Howl*
I try again as I spark
a joint, hotbox the Silver
Bullet Calivan. Silsbe
reaches for the Van Morrison cd
we play the first track or two
then he says *alright let's get right
to it* and plays *Almost Independence Day*
we talk about all his guttural
moaning, his interjections, his
ejaculations as he sings, it's impossible
to replicate, it's always overdone
it's always perfect. today though
it's the title track of *St Dominic's Preview*
that's put a nail in my heart, when Van sings
everybody feels so determined not to feel anyone else's pain

we walk through a cloud of vapor smoke
the barista seems confused
Borczon talks about the naval reserve
with the Syrian chemical weapons strike his people
clamor for answers, there's a storm

coming, perhaps a war about to dawn
I hear your poems now Matt and I think
this is not about what you've already seen
this about dread, a premonition of what
you'll see, what we will all may see again
whether live, on the news, in our living rooms
he remembers talking to a group of soldiers
reminding them democracy is something
you fight for, but don't mistake this as a democracy

Van and the road have me thinking about
America, I was in a house that was a stop
on the Underground Railroad this morning
with this administration, I think more
on the meaning of freedom than I have
before, I see coming wars as good
for business, good for a cabal of
rich white men, they have no concern
for us, for the citizens of an alleged democracy

I'm in a bar with Stolte,
his lady and Silsbe and there
are paintings of Jimmy Stewart movies
hanging, Stolte is not familiar with *Harvey*
one of my maternal grandmother's favorite
movies, and now one of mine

it seems democracy is a Pooka
something imaginary, something like
a six-foot eight rabbit that all but
a few can actually see

A Cheeseburger on Memorial Day

I order a cheeseburger
and fries at the Middle
Eastern market cafeteria
cause it's Memorial Day

Memorial Day
or Decoration Day
a lip service holiday
for those that gave
what is known patriotically
as the ultimate sacrifice

I enjoyed my cheeseburger
on Memorial Day, during Ramadan,
when Muslims fast till sunset, I wanted
to celebrate immigrants
and the possibilities
of a world without hate
a world where no one dies in wars
a world that doesn't exist
because of U.S. foreign policy

I thought as I finished my cheeseburger
on Memorial Day, of all the flags
planted like seeds in cemeteries that bloom in May
how it wouldn't take more than
a strong wind to blow all those flags away

Elegy for the American Dream

it's not when, it's if the car starts
it's when the bill comes due
you realize no matter how much
you worked, it ain't enough
it's when they say *go to the doctor*
but you don't have insurance
even if you did there's a deductible
it's going to work so sick you can't
stand up but you can't miss the pay
it's threatening yourself with the free clinic
if you don't get better
it's choosing the gas bill
or the electric bill this week
it's trying to stretch two meals
out of everything
it's standing for hours in long lines to drop off paperwork
for food stamps only to get the interview
and find you make $50 more than the cut-off
it's peanut butter sandwiches
it's grilled cheese sandwiches
every night, because you bought
that loaf of bread and you can't even
let the ends go to waste
it's shoplifting milk
it's making forty dollars last two weeks
it's counting quarters to buy gas
it's counting quarters to buy detergent

it's counting quarters till payday
it's chasing after your pay
it's called being cash strapped
it's the rent always being due
it's the collection agency on the phone
at eight am everyday
so you never need an alarm clock
it's realizing that minimum wage
means you mean nothing
it's a ten-cent raise, or a quarter raise
or a percentage raise that barely
adds up to an extra $20 in pay after taxes
it's having your debit card stolen
and everything bounces
it's feeling rich when you get your tax
return only to be broke the next day
it's always bottom shelf or in a box
it's not buying things new until the old is broken
even then, it's trying to get by broken
it's regretting every unnecessary transaction
it's counting wasted time
it's being too stressed to do anything other than waste time
it's the two-job exhaustion
it's not saying no to cash side work or overtime
it's someone telling you to pull
yourself up from your boot straps
when you can't get a break
it's you telling them fuck off
because they never needed one

Hymn to Conspiracies

I work for a plumber now and again
we talk politics sometimes
he states he's fiscally conservative
while socially liberal
a decade and change older than me
we see the world differently
I haven't identified myself as socialist
I think it's known

I spent a day talking to him about redlining
a practice in effect for eighty years
I mention the civil rights movement
how MK Ultra undermined radical change
in this country in the sixties
I talk about how heroin was nearly eradicated
after World War II, only to be reintroduced
by the CIA as Vietnam was escalated
I talk about urban renewal, the war on drugs
how heroin, then crack, were used to destroy
the black community
how mass incarceration destroyed black family structure
how those same tactics are now being used
in poor white communities by pharmaceutical companies
in an opioid epidemic that's really
another in a long line of policies
by the rich to keep control of their interests

it's their country not ours, it's a democracy
loosely speaking, but it's not democratic
for those of us looking up

we have been trained to want
to want what we don't have
to blame those below us
for taking from us, not those
above us who continue to squeeze
those of us who are poor out

he doesn't believe me

I didn't get into
fringe conspiracies like
9/11 was an inside job
even though you can watch the rise
of fascism come from that ugly
day, from that fucking root

I didn't get to shock doctrine
or how the Kennedy Assassination was
engineered by the CIA and the Mafia or Eisenhower's
warning about the Military Industrial Complex

I didn't even try the farthest fringes
the laughable from way out
John Titor and alien conquest

reptiles from the 4th dimension
the lost planet of Nibiru or Agenda 21

all of the information I presented
is easily findable, most of it now mainstream
he still didn't believe me

days later we're working
I make inflammatory comments
about our corporate masters
he says *do you hate all rich people*
he says it to me as if I used a racial epithet

I say *yes*

A Hymn for the Surveillance State

walking into the dollar store
sign on the door says
*this location is under video
surveillance for your protection
         for your safety*

I see these signs more often
it's like they weren't here
then like magic they are

safety is an illusion
our lives and the world
we live in are reflections
of the universe we live in
and the universe is chaos

we try and make order
from chaos in order
to make sense of our lives
we believe we have control
but the reality is simple
we only have a modicum of control

the reality is simple
this is a police state
this is a surveillance state

fascism and totalitarianism
are in full bloom

we trade freedom
we trade our rights
for the illusion of safety

as humans
we are free
as Americans
we are decidedly not free

Postcard from Kimberling Lake

you know the ordeal is almost over
you followed the cop's finger
as a UFO in the dark, flashlight
burning your eyes, you blew
.00 he asks again
*what are you doing
in this part of Missouri?*

you know from the moment
he pulled you over for a line
violation that he was fishing
saw out of state plates
thought he may turn up
something more
now they're trying that other tactic
where they look
for inconsistencies in your story

you know stories grow upon each retell
details grow with ownership
he's turned the flashlight off
this last question will get you
back on the road, you wish
you could see his eyes
when you answer
you're a poet

you shake his hand as you head back
to the car, this is a police state
this is Missouri which is now
the Show Me Your ID State

To My Poet Friends on an American Holy Day

Ally, your new manuscript
is a candle inside
my heart to keep loss away
even a blurb is not enough
to say how much those words
meant as they scraped against
memory and bone

but I appreciate all the manuscripts
I recently finished advances of Borczon and Clevenger
deep riots felt in the ridges of the heart

I think of poems Nikki, Renee
and I construct via text
I think of Julio's birthday greetings
his request: if I had any wishes
he would happily drop
them in the Grand Canyon

we gathered as friends
on an American holy day
laughing, sharing
a little heavy from the drink
it's always a joy to hear Silsbe's work
today it's his New Kids on the Block story
complete with lascivious dancing

and self-groping, or Pajich
the way he vibrates when
he tells stories, or to have Irwin's
hand on my shoulder to steady
himself as he laughs in that
distinct staccato way or
Collins' quiet calm turning every poem
into an ocean you'll never see all of

I consider voice
I read everyday even if
it's a poem or two online
maybe one of Grochalski's gruff right hooks
or Benger's trailer park psalms
or some deep voice of the past
say William Wantling or Jack Micheline
Li Po or Hikmet, so many more
so many people inspire me

I read now because I can't be without
those voices
those voices steer me
keep me steady

it seems to me those voices
weird and disparate, my poet friends
these oddball mystic wanderers
in every corner of this bloated
dying experiment of America

we shout
some deep consciousness
some lost empathy
we want others to believe
this America is an appropriation
of a dream, it's not the America
we ever believed it should be

On finding Three Hundred Dollars in a Book on FDR That I Ordered off the Internet

(For Lori Jakiela)

thank you
FDR
for paying
my rent
this month

Lunch Time, Spahr Avenue

he says I'm not prejudiced
but I really hate the Indians at 7-11
how the government gives them money
to come here and open up stores
I say sorry brother I never heard that one before

over lunch, he says how much Jews bother him
asks if I'm Jewish, today we work for a Jewish family
I tell him it's possible, I don't know for sure
I don't have money for the genetics test
but a limited family history
suggests it's more than possible

I say my best friend is Jewish
I really don't know how you tell
a Jew from a Gentile
they look about the same to me
can you define how you tell them apart?
he can't, he says something else
another racial epithet, he's used a few today

I say, dude, far as I see
people are just that, people
humans are human
you got a few jagoffs, but mostly
I've been lucky to know good people

and good people, can't be defined by race
we are human, culturally we're different
racially we may be different but when
it comes down to it, who really cares
we're all just human

he shakes his head, says again
he's not prejudiced, I just don't like
people, hell, I don't like myself

Beefeaters

I found the new
American metaphor

in a steakhouse
formerly a library
with a few books for decor

stereo sits crooked
on milk crate

wait staff
outnumbers patrons

haven't seen
the bartender
in 20 minutes

outside there used to be
oil and aircraft
at least there's still lighters

outside there used to be

I feel like John Wayne
over budget, overfed

high on red meat
naked without a pistol

on a road everyone forgot

Postcard from Bunker Hill

roadside sign says
bunker hill
shoot out
tickets
$10
as if
all of
America
isn't already
why buy
a ticket?

Another Day in America

there's a man on Douglas
looking up at the sky
as I get closer, he makes
eye contact says
*have you ever seen
anything like that?*
points at three helicopters
triangulating
he says there was a gunfight
on the street corner
over the hill
the choppers
are looking
for the shooter
he wonders
how they'll find them

I nod, think about a friend
who texted this afternoon
said her building was on lockdown
an active shooter situation outside

it should be disturbing
but this is just another
day in America

Supplemental Nights

minor regional poet, the end of town
the dust of modernity clouds over the lights
of a thousand lost art deco bulbs

almost show time, why not
maybe this is better than burying
oneself in a rathskeller
waiting out the apocalypse

a cavern for three
so much time to stand still
projector rolls shaky
white lights to images
another apocalypse

all this dystopian entertainment
images of war, man vs man, man vs state
man vs supernatural, man as superhero

as if to say that the world you live in
isn't that bad, there's worse
there will be worse to come
please rationalize the Orwellian fantasy
you prefer, let it take your mind off
your current Orwellian fantasy

there are monkeys on screen
who take over the world
maybe the rathskeller
the sweat of a bottle, summer heat
would have been preferable

I leave the last picture show
I still hear it

the horror
the horror
the horror

Onagrocracy
(for John Grochalski)

christ I'm discouraged
Jay, I know exactly how you feel
we knew it wouldn't be
four years of winning
maybe we thought shit
would get worse more quickly
but this banana republic
can't tell its ass
from a hole in the ground

I don't know why worse quickly
would have been better
maybe after the hell of 2016
we were up for a fight
blood up after a slash and burn election

instead it's been a barrage of ineptitude
things getting worse but slowly
a barrage of policy changes
some in secret, some in the open
some buried on Friday so not to
ruffle the feathers of the nightly news

it's hard to keep the outrage up
when everything is outrageous
everything is this is not my country
everything is *hey America*
you could have had a real democracy

there's a term from Fascist Italy
Onagrocracy, it loosely translates
to a government of braying asses
to say that one must acknowledge
the tumble down to Fascism
America has become
maybe we're too late
maybe we woke up too late

christ, I'm discouraged too
I wonder why I care this much
a country is fiction, we all bought in
even as we learned to take each
Horatio Alger American Dream
platitude as the lies they are

christ I'm discouraged
I still got a bad case
of *it can't happen here*
even as it happens here

Jay, I know you're discouraged
goddamn, so am I

but we still need our voices
we still got a fight
or try to fight the ways we know how
we still have to believe in the ballot
if there was any mistake it was
teaching us that was the truth
if we give up
then democracy
is rehearsing
for retirement

Hymn to the Greatest

I pulled into the goodwill
the one near the college
the one near the wal-mart
the one across the highway from a convenience store
the one down the highway from two more convenience stores
the one overlooking the nuclear power plant
the one right where the incline to the highlands starts

the car cd player is broken
scan the dial on the radio
I rest on the right-wing nut
    the guy filling in for Savage
    the guy whose anti-Muslim rhetoric is nauseating
    the guy that says America is the greatest country in the world

I wonder momentarily about the greatest country in the world
was there a vote, a quorum, did a group of countries
get together and sing *He's a Jolly Good Fellow*
then give us a wrist watch for our service
talk about how they want to be great countries too

we should probably be suspicious
of anyone American who says
this is the greatest country
it isn't, I don't know off my head
that I would hand that award out to any country
a country is as good as the people it contains

it is a reflection of the attitudes of those people
it is also wholly imaginary, man made
like time, like god, like boundaries, like dreams

to ballyhoo is propaganda
it obfuscates the real conversation
the fact that to question, to challenge
the normalcy of any government
is patriotism, it's required
for any country to be the
proper reflection of its people

to say you're the greatest
without proof, without basis
is to be a child

god forbid
we are a nation
of children

Talking God with Ussia

we agree the christian right is neither
it's more of a terrorist organization
I say *I don't understand how we
try to apply a two-thousand-year-old morality
to this fleeting concept of modernity*

Ussia says *what's up with heaven as a concept
after you die you go somewhere where
everyone you love is now and you're there for eternity
personally, that sounds like hell* I say

we both comment on an antiquated god in the face of science
thinking that our concept of god, like the universe, or eternity
is faulty, there's no way to apply humanity to it
humanity is a value that still can't be quantified

A Fedora and a Mustache

referenced by her brother-in-law
she calls, leaves an awkward
voice message, walking around
what she wants or needs

I listen already somewhat amused
I deal in edible marijuana
not much, enough for friends
enough to take a little off the top
to pay for my own indulgence
because fuck it, sometimes,
no, all the time, this world is too much
we need the edge off

she is in her late fifties, I think
her husband has cancer
she like me in an untenable space
she's never done a drug deal
I hate thinking of myself
as a drug dealer

I buy cookies from cancer patients
I sell cookies to people with anxiety
chronic pain, cancer or to people
who just want to have a good time

marijuana helps these things
marijuana should be legal
we should all be able to walk into a dispensary
pick up what we need, not through
some underground economy
fuck you America, for making us criminals

a friend of mine died of cancer last year
the pain killers were too much
until the pain got too bad
then there was no choice but painkillers
until that point though
I showed him how to roll joints
how to pack a bong
how to smoke
'cause these aren't cigarettes

she's much the same, nervous as she talks
she says *can I say cookies, will alarm bells
ring, will I be arrested immediately*
I start to laugh, laugh through the rest
of the conversation, she says
*this was something you didn't
do in my day, the fear of jail was too much*
I tell her it's been decriminalized in the city
even as this archaic government
tries its best now to double down
on what has been proven to be

a far less dangerous drug
than alcohol, cigarettes or caffeine

we set up a meeting, she asks
should I wear a disguise, I could
fedora, I could mustache
I could fake glasses
I say *there's no need*
we don't want to draw attention
we want to make this fast and painless

she calls back to change the meeting
I'm going to her house now
she tells me the address
she tells me to look for the house
wearing a fedora and mustache

For Trane's Giant Steps

the traffic lights on Western
change from solid to blinking
at eleven every night

I hit Liberty
race through the Strip
windows down, heat on
the first winter night
John Coltrane's *Giant Steps*
blares, I'm not irritated
Jimmy Garrison's bass clips
from the radio tower

I drift through this nights
free Oberon pitchers
the lonely pit bull terrier
the frat dudes working
as an assembly line
on a teener of cocaine

I sit with the lawyers
hypothetically solving
the world's problems

it's been a year since the coronation
of a madman, of a clearly transparent
puppet of a class of oligarchs
somehow, we've yet to sink to oblivion
even as each day becomes
another crisis for a non-existent democracy

as the first clear waves
of resistance come into view
all the wasted narratives
of what is America
ring more hollow than ever

Mr Pink Pussy Hat Salesman

I noticed you at the women's march
as we all prepared to walk
you on the fringe of the crowd
a rolling cart of pink pussy hats
anti-trump stickers, paraphernalia

I noticed you again
as we marched
our pace slow through
Pittsburgh city streets
you galloped along
pink hats shaking
as you tried, tried again
at another sale

I noticed you one last time
as the speakers finished up
marchers returned to wherever
standing on the corner
selling a hat, selling a sticker
maybe it's not fair
to believe I could find you
as easily at a Trump rally
selling hats and t-shirts
Make America Great Again

maybe it's not fair
but I realize simply
Capitalism
has no allegiance

Three Views of High Street

walking down High Street
after dinner, holding
hands, there's a homeless
man and a passerby
he's holding the homeless
man's hand, eyes closed
saying a prayer
I want to say
god doesn't exist
and I'm tired
of people thinking
thoughts and prayers
are enough

we talk on the way
to a bar about
what a wreck
West Virginia has become
or always was
I say it's the coal operators
who've fucked this state
they've taken
huge fortunes on the backs
of broken workers, at the expense
of these state's citizens

at the expense of this state's
natural beauty. you know
this is the only state where
bombs were dropped
by the military on striking
miners, that was barely
one hundred years ago

later, in bed on the sixth
floor of what used to be
a fancy hotel,
quiet talk
the sirens flow constant
she says half serious
we should get married
so you have health insurance
I laugh almost a full minute
finally say *if you throw in*
your dental plan
I'll consider it
she says, *what is marriage*
good for if not insurance
I say, *I guess, but it's fucked*
we have to think that way

The Hymn to Blood Sport

they drive beamers, porsches and hummers
up northumberland to the golf course
they don't stop for working men
doesn't matter the weight they carry
or that it's ninety degrees outside
they see a worker, they speed up

I have twenty boxes of books
to drop at the local library
nothing exciting, but cheap
and saleable. the guy who's
about my age is excited
all the boxes are uniform
they'll fit in storage easily

I bring the last dollyful
he says, *do you think there
are any part time jobs open?*
I laugh, *I am the part time job*

as if keeping your job
is now a blood sport
he answers back, *you're bigger than me
you can keep the job*

I walk to the van. he says
funny isn't it, all there is is
part time work. I laugh
I have four part time jobs
I juggle. he looks at me
do you think we'll make it to seventy?
I answer quickly, *fuck no!*
it's always hard not to swear
I say, *pardon me if that's harsh*
but fuck no. he laughs, says
if I wasn't working, I'd say the same damn thing

March of the Infidels

it's rained hard
torrential, no visibility
for all but nine
of the last sixty miles

off the highway
greeted by an embankment
covered in small flags
looking like
two hundred and fifty
tiny desk sets
two flags, four blades
of grass, forever patriotic

on the stereo
Bud Powell plays
March of the Infidels
staccato intro
before the head
comes in full swing

Bud, you and I
are infidels
all these flags
tokens of some patriotic

religion, some zeitgeist
where it is no longer
patriotic to question
the rule of law

you were beaten
unconscious by Philadelphia
police in 1945
you heard voices
for the rest of his life

I live in a time
where cops still do their best
to kill black men in the streets

I'm waiting on some voice
to bring sanity to
to a country that's teetering

I'm waiting on some voice
that, like your fingers
across the keys of a piano
still celebrates humanity

Kerouac Go Home

I hear the waitress' footfalls
they sound like roses as they echo
across Avenue B, as they echo
across the Avenue of the Americas
they echo at the intersection of Bleeker
& McDougal where Silsbe can't understand
why there's so many people, sure
he's got a few drinks in him
but I never thought I'd see New Yorkers
turn heads at open indictments of procreation
or at least procreation with the intent
to further the fading bulb of humanity

Jay and Ally say they used to write
Kerouac Go Home on the men's room
wall at the White Horse
Dylan Thomas is bleeding out
the blood trail runs to the Chelsea Hotel
then beyond. I slipped on it when I tried to
remember the last time I had a future

I tried to remember the last time
I saw the ocean, there were mustangs
racing on the Garden State Parkway
there were little hands waving on BQE

I swear there was a liberty torch
in the harbor, its head
struggling above the surface

I've snagged myself, a driftwood
sculpture, there is so much debris
the gulls have picked through
the soft shelled and horseshoe crabs
the few untouched are boiling
to burst, but the ocean it still
waves under the twin eyes of lighthouses
it never bothered with magic or loss

Jason Baldinger is a poet hailing from Pittsburgh and recently finished a stint as writer in residence at the Osage Arts Community. He is co-director of The Bridge Series reading series. He's the author of several books, the most recent are *This Useless Beauty* (Alien Buddha Press), *The Ugly Side of the Lake* (NightBallet Press) written with John Dorsey and the chaplet *Fumbles Revelations* (Grackle and Crow) which are available now. The collection *Fragments of a Rainy Season* (Six Gallery Press) and the split book with James Benger, *Little Fires Hiding* (Kung Fu Treachery Press) are forthcoming. Recent publications include the *Low Ghost Anthology Unconditional Surrender, The Dope Fiend Daily, Outlaw Poetry, Uppagus, Lilliput*

Review, Rusty Truck, Dirtbag Review, In Between Hangovers, Your One Phone Call, Winedrunk Sidewalk, Anti-Heroin Chic, Nerve Cowboy Concrete Meat Press, Zombie Logic Press, Ramingo's Porch, Rye Whiskey Review, Red Fez, Mad Swirl, Blue Hour Review and *Heartland! Poetry of Love, Solidarity and Resistance.* You can hear Jason read poems on recent and forthcoming releases by Theremonster and Sub Pop Recording artist The Gotobeds as well as at jasonbaldinger.bandcamp.com

www.ingramcontent.com/pod-product-compliance
Lightning Source LLC
Chambersburg PA
CBHW020127130526
44591CB00032B/556